Wild Weather

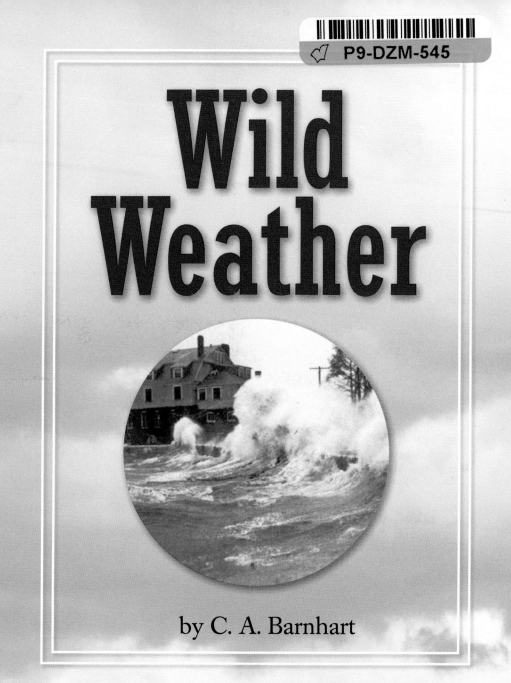

by C. A. Barnhart

PEARSON

Scott
Foresman

Editorial Offices: Glenview, Illinois • Parsippany, New Jersey • New York, New York
Sales Offices: Needham, Massachusetts • Duluth, Georgia • Glenview, Illinois
Coppell, Texas • Ontario, California • Mesa, Arizona

Weather

If you were an astronaut gazing at Earth from your spacecraft, Earth and the space around it would look very clear, like a multicolored ball hanging in front of a dark backdrop. What if you looked at a picture of Earth taken from a satellite? A satellite orbits Earth at a lower level than the astronaut. It would show only one part of Earth at a time. From this point of view, Earth looks as if it is shrouded in a veil, the atmosphere. As your space camera approaches Earth, you can see clouds and clear spaces that make up the large swirling masses that determine the weather we experience on the ground.

People always want to know what the weather will be. Sailors and farmers are especially affected by weather, and long ago, being able to "read" the clouds, winds, and sky was a valuable skill. These practical weathermen understood enough about the weather to recognize winds that could cause trouble. They might not have been able to attach names to clouds, for example, but they would know that thin clouds high in the sky would signal a change coming. Today we know these as **cirrus** clouds.

Earth as seen from space

The name **cumulus** might not have meant anything to our practical weathermen, but when they saw cumulus clouds floating up in the sky like cotton balls, they knew they could expect fair weather. If cumulus clouds became darker in color and piled up in the sky, a thunderstorm was brewing. **Stratus** clouds, which look like flat, wrinkled gray sheets lying across the sky, can indicate snow in cold weather or rain in warmer weather. A wind from a certain direction could bring a storm.

The difficulty for our early practical forecasters, however, was that they based their forecasts on what they could see at that moment. They did not have much time to prepare for either good weather or dangerous storms. Farmers and sailors, in particular, recognized which cloud formations signaled a simple a change in weather or an approaching storm. But the advance warning they got from "reading" the clouds would have only given them several hours' notice. Today **meteorology,** the science of weather, has been helped a great deal by advances in technology.

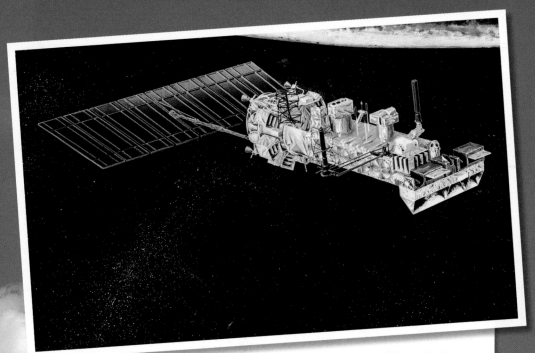

Weather satellites help meteorologists make forecasts.

Meteorologists rely on **radar** images, or images sent from weather satellites, to observe masses of air, the high and low pressure areas that create the weather we experience on Earth. Meteorologists send up weather balloons to measure temperature, pressure, and wind levels high in the atmosphere. By collecting this data, meteorologists can estimate the kind of weather that is likely to affect a large or small area of Earth for a whole season, not just the next few days.

By recording weather information in computer databases, meteorologists can compare it with data collected from the past. This means that weather forecasts are based on actual temperature, wind, humidity, and pressure readings taken from both high in the atmosphere and closer to the ground. Forecasters can also study weather occurring one place in the atmosphere that may eventually affect weather in another distant place.

Space technology has also helped with forecasting the weather. Long ago, a scientist might have wished to fly high above the weather to see what it looked like before it reached a certain place on Earth. Through space technology, meteorologists observe air masses in the atmosphere, which means that meteorologists can look at the weather from above the clouds.

Understanding and planning for weather is important to everyone. Airlines need to know if the weather will cause problems with the flights they have scheduled, and a ship's captain must know what the weather will be like in order to plot a safe course across an ocean. Local and state governments need to know when a serious storm is approaching so that people can be warned and protect themselves from its effects. Families also want to know what the weather is going to be like when they are planning a picnic or hoping to attend a baseball game.

Technology helps meteorologists forecast the weather.

The Hurricane of 1938

Planes used to drop hurricane warnings
to fishermen in their boats.

Even long ago, before forecasters had radar,
satellites, and computers to help them predict the
direction and force of a storm, people who lived
along the southeastern coast would expect hurricanes
between June and November. However, where
hurricanes were rare, it was a very different situation.
In 1938, toward the end of September, a hurricane
raced up the eastern coast of the United States, tore
across Long Island, New York, and then went straight
north into New England.

It is not often that hurricanes travel to the northeastern part of the United States. Usually, hurricanes lose their force before they reach New England, and before they can bring strong, gusty winds and high tides, which can cause some flooding and damage. Most of the time, storms in New England are not considered life-threatening weather events, unlike major hurricanes.

The United States Weather Bureau knew about the hurricane of 1938 before it was supposed to hit the western coast of Florida. Because of weather conditions in the southern part of the country, however, the storm turned eastward and seemed to be heading out into the Atlantic Ocean. Since forecasters knew that the last major hurricane to hit New England was in 1869, it seemed unlikely that this hurricane would travel inland.

The destruction caused by hurricanes can take many lives.

This couple sits in what is left of their
home after the hurricane of 1938.

A high-pressure air mass stationed over the Atlantic
Ocean was blocking the storm from moving out to sea.
The conditions were just right for the hurricane to be
drawn along the East Coast, across Long Island, and
inland through New England. The storm kept moving
north at more than fifty miles per hour!

The hurricane of 1938 was the most powerful storm
that New Englanders had ever experienced. It was a
Category 3 hurricane with winds gusting over 180
miles per hour. Hurricanes are classified from 1 to 5
according to severity–5 being the most severe. The
hurricane downed power lines. Trees were uprooted,
roads were washed out, and bridges were destroyed.
Since people did not know the hurricane of 1938
was coming, there was not enough time for them to
evacuate, and hundreds of people were killed.

People who survived the hurricane of 1938 were grateful, and some people wrote articles or letters about what they saw and felt while the storm raged around them. Some people survived the storm by clinging to the roofs of their houses. Some people watched as their homes were blown apart and carried off by the **surge** of water that came ashore with the hurricane. No one ever wanted to get caught in a storm like that again!

Young girls rummage through the hurricane-damaged remains of their home.

Hurricane Charley (2004)

If you lived in Florida in the summer of 2004, you will remember Hurricane Charley. Meteorologists spotted Hurricane Charley in the South Atlantic long before it reached Florida. Their warnings stated that Charley would be at least a Category 3 hurricane, striking with heavy rain and winds of up to 130 miles per hour.

Another danger was that Charley might create a great storm surge, which would cause flooding in many coastal areas. Many people packed bags and left their homes, while others made plans to stay in emergency shelters where they would be safe. Anyone living close to the water was forced to leave. Shopkeepers had to board up windows to prevent them from being shattered by Charley's strong winds.

As things turned out, Charley was a Category 4 hurricane with winds as powerful as 155 miles per hour! It struck Florida's west coast and sped across the state, causing great damage. The hurricane uprooted trees and snapped them in two, smashed mobile homes, and flooded buildings.

Hurricane Charley blew roofs off homes, collapsed walls, and shattered windows. In some places the electricity went out, and there was no running water. Hurricane Charley tossed cars into the air as if they were toys. As bad as Charley was, though, there was less destruction and loss of life than if there hadn't been weather predictions, as in the hurricane of 1938. Because they were warned, people expected Hurricane Charley and had time to prepare.

Hurricane Charley near the southern tip of Florida (above) and the destruction it caused (left)

The Great White Hurricane of 1888

Because it lies next to the ocean, the eastern coast of the United States gets many heavy snow and rain storms. As a storm system moves across water, it picks up moisture and becomes stronger. If such a storm happens along with very cold temperatures, the result is a huge snowstorm. Storms that have heavy snowfall, strong winds, and cold temperatures are called blizzards, and they can last two or more days.

The Great White Hurricane was one such historic blizzard. It occurred in March 1888 and affected the entire East Coast of the United States from Maryland to Maine. It lasted for three days, unleashing more than four feet of snow on New York City, and nearly five feet of snow on New England. Winds caused the snow to blow into tall drifts, with some drifts reaching as high as second-story windows!

The blizzard of '88 came on so quickly that New Yorkers were caught unprepared. The storm began late on a Sunday night in March. The weather had been warm, and residents thought that the storm would pass. On Monday morning, many people left their homes to go to work, but the storm got worse and worse. Some people were stranded at work, while others tried to walk home through the blinding snow.

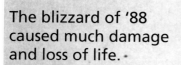

The blizzard of '88 caused much damage and loss of life.

Trains, taxis, and ferry boats were unable to run. In fact, the storm stopped trains from going in and out of Grand Central Station. New York City, one of the busiest cities in the world, came to a halt, and it took many days for the city to get back on its feet. One result of the Great White Hurricane was that New York City decided to build a subway system so that the city would never again be paralyzed by a storm.

The Storm of the Century (1993)

More than one hundred years later, in 1993, the eastern United States experienced another blizzard. Some people called it the "Storm of the Century." This storm hit the entire eastern part of the United States, from Maine to Florida, and almost half of the country was affected in some way.

Heavy snow fell on parts of the southeast, an area that rarely receives even a light dusting of snow. In Tennessee, fifty-six inches fell in one place, while Birmingham, Alabama, measured six-foot snowdrifts. In northern Florida, several inches of snow fell, and high winds caused damage similar to the kind caused by a hurricane.

A woman digs out her snowed-in car.

People on their way to work climb over piles of ice and snow.

Every large airport on the East Coast was shut down. High winds and fallen trees downed power lines, and heavy snow collected on rooftops, which caused some buildings to collapse. Millions of people were without electricity, which meant that they did not have heat.

Sophisticated computers helped meteorologists recognize that this was not an ordinary storm. Meteorologists issued storm warnings to all the areas likely to be in the path of the Storm of the Century. In most cases, people stayed in the safety of their own homes. Since most people were warned about the storm, they were able to prepare for it.

These serious storms are exciting to read about, and, if you are in a safe place, they are exciting to witness. For those who are injured or who have lost their homes, a storm is something they will never forget.

Dust Storms of the 1930s

But what can anyone do about a kind of storm that lasts for nearly ten years?

More than seventy years ago, severe **drought** struck five states in the Great Plains and Southwest. There was little rainfall, so the soil became very dry and blew away in high winds. The drought lasted for nearly ten years and caused thousands of farmers to leave the area. When too little rain falls on unplanted, unprotected land, blowing wind can create **dust storms.** Because dust storms happen often in this area, it is known as the dust bowl.

During a dust storm, particles of dirt are carried by the wind, and sometimes the wind carries so much dust that people are blinded and choked by the whirling particles. The sky darkens, and the blowing dust enters a house or barn through any little crack or opening. During this period of drought and dust storms, dust bowl farmers lost their farms, animals, and all their savings.

Today, farmers plant lines of trees to break up the winds. Then the winds are less likely to **erode** the soil. Today, instead of planting crops in the dust bowl, farmers use the land as grassland and pasture for cattle.

DUST STORM APPROACHING SPEARMAN, TEXAS.
APRIL 14, 1935

Clouds of dirt in a dust storm

These houses in Texas are about
to get hit by a dust storm.

Hurricane

Blizzard

Dust storm

As you can see, the forces of nature can be fierce, and it is important to be prepared when severe weather is expected. Hurricanes, blizzards, and dust storms have destroyed homes and communities, as well as taken lives. The damage caused by strong winds, crashing waves, blinding snow, or whirling dust may have been repaired over time, but people who have lived through severe weather will never forget their experiences.

Technology has helped meteorologists predict storms so that people can be prepared before danger strikes. That is why being able to view Earth from above the clouds is so important.

Extreme weather conditions and events make good stories. While storms can be as exciting as frightening movies, they are real, and they are uncontrollable. Through technology, we have been able to predict when wild weather is on its way. As we learn more about our weather, we can reduce the amount of destruction that great weather events can cause.

Be a Weather Historian

Do you like rainy days? Does snow make you happy? Do you like days that are sunny and clear? No matter how you feel about the weather, you cannot do anything to change it, but you can find out more about the weather by being a weather historian.

The Great White
Hurricane of 1888

1. Keep a weather diary where you describe the weather each day. Be sure to write about interesting changes in the weather. Include how you reacted, what you felt, or what you noticed about the weather on a particular day.

2. Write a history of storms where you live. Your local paper should have articles from the past about storm events. Ask older people in your community if they remember an especially serious weather event. Record their stories in your diary.

3. Look for pictures of past storms and include them in your diary or history. Add pictures of places that still show signs of earlier storm damage, such as a photo of a building, a stand of trees, or a beach area.

4. Once you've collected some weather history, decorate your notebook. Make sure that you've included pictures showing the effects of big storms. Share your weather history with classmates, and learn more from their reports about the weather where you live.

Glossary

category *n.* (used with numbers 1–5) a classification of the severity of hurricanes.

cirrus *n.* a high cloud formation that is thin and feathery in appearance.

cumulus *n.* a puffy cloud formation that is round at the top and flat on the bottom.

drought *n.* a long period of too little rainfall.

dust storms *n.* windstorms that carry small particles of dirt from a dry area.

erode *v.* to wear away.

meteorology *n.* the science or study of weather.

radar *n.* a machine or system for measuring the distance, direction, speed, etc., of unseen objects by the reflection of microwave radio patterns.

stratus *n.* a flat, gray sheet of clouds that spreads over a large area.

surge *n.* a sudden or violent rushing wave of water.